# Up and down

# A shade
# can go up.

# A shade
# can come down.

# A ladder can go up.

# A ladder

# can come down.

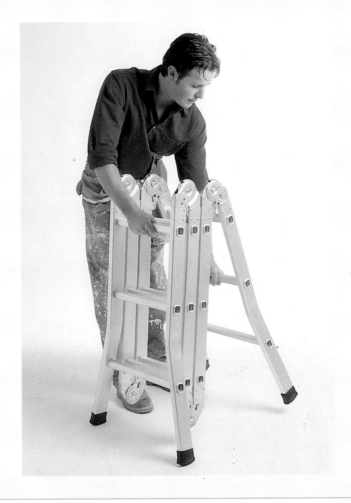

# An umbrella
# can go up.

# An umbrella can come down.

# A flying fox
# can go up.

# A flying fox
# can come down.

# An escalator can go up.

# An escalator

# can come down.

# An elevator
# can go up.

# An elevator
# can come down.

A helicopter
can go up.

A helicopter

can come down.

I can go up,

and I can come down.

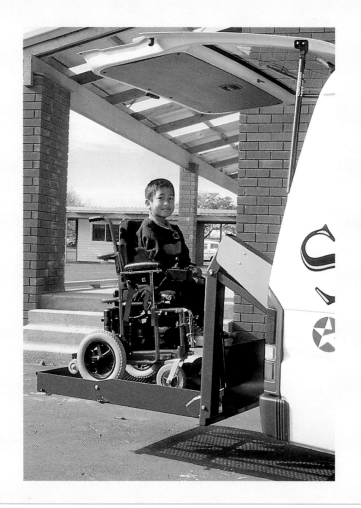